THE HEARTBEAT OF FAITH

Fifty-Nine Poems, Fingerplays, and Prayers
Preschool-Early Primary

Mary Kathleen Glavich, SND

THE HEARTBEAT OF FAITH
Fifty-Nine Poems, Fingerplays, and Prayers
Mary Kathleen Glavich, SND

Cover design and typesetting by Patricia A. Lynch
Illustrations by Mary Kathleen Glavich, SND
Published by ACTA Publications, 4848 N. Clark St.,
Chicago, IL 60640, (800) 397-2282, actapublications.com

Library of Congress Control Number: 2016946893
ISBN: 978-0-87946-579-7
Printed in the United States of America by Total Printing Systems
Year 25 24 23 22 21 20 19 18 17 16
Printing 12 11 10 9 8 7 6 5 4 3 2 First

✪ Text printed on 30% post-consumer recycled paper

CONTENTS

INTRODUCTION

Children may turn up their noses at broccoli, but what about poetry? Both are good for them, but thankfully they **love** poetry. As little children hear or, better still, recite poems, they develop a sense of language. The rhymes introduce them to phonics, and the words and phrases increase their vocabulary. Children seem to be born with an appetite for rhyme, rhythm, and repetition. Perhaps the steady rhythm of poetry reminds them of their mother's heartbeat.

Poetry makes an excellent vehicle not only for conveying concepts, but for forming values and virtues. **The Heartbeat of Faith** offers poems that have an extra benefit: They nurture faith.

Some of the poems in this collection give children an understanding of God as their maker, who loves and cares about them. Others introduce them to the importance of loving others; teach them how to pray; and lay the foundation for a relationship with Jesus, Mary, and the angels and an appreciation of the Bible and Christian feast days. A "We Talk" for each poem includes questions for discussion.

I know firsthand the effectiveness of poems and fingerplays. As a first grade teacher, I was amazed how quickly the children memorized a verse, while I had to rely on a written copy. They never tired of poems and songs that were accompanied by gestures and movements, but two performances of "Head, Shoulders, Knees, and Toes" was all I could bear.

Chances are that you can still recite nursery rhymes and sing camp songs that you learned as a tot. Maybe even now you sing the little song or recite the verse that helps us remember the number of days in each month.

Parents, grandparents, and teachers will find this book a delightful source of entertainment, instruction, and faith formation for the children in their care. Someday, the children may wish to read the poems for themselves. But then again, they might already know them all by heart!

Mary Kathleen Glavich, SND

ME AND MY FAMILY

I AM SPECIAL

To the tune of "Twinkle, Twinkle, Little Star"

Twinkle, twinkle, little star,
[Open and close fists raised high.]
God has made us what we are.

Though a million stars I see,
[Sweep arms from left to right.]
You are special just like me.
[Point thumb at self.]

Twinkle, twinkle, little star,
[Open and close fists raised high.]
God has made us what we are.

WE TALK

No two people are alike, not even identical twins.

• How are you different from other children?
• What special things can you do?

Growing Up

When I was a baby,
I was very, very small.
[Stoop and be as small as possible.]

Today I am just this size.
[Stand and place hand on top of head.]

And someday I'll be tall.
[Stretch hands high.]

WE TALK

Eating good food helps us grow and be healthy.

• How tall are you?
• How much do you weigh?
• How can you tell that you are growing?
• What can you do now that you couldn't do
  when you were a baby?

My Nose

With my nose I smell things like these:
Bacon, popcorn, and Christmas trees,
Babies, roses, and apple pie.
And this is probably the reason why
My nose has such an important place —
Right in the middle of my face.

WE TALK

Noses help us taste food. When you have a cold and can't smell, you can't taste your food. Noses also protect us. They tell us when something is burning. They let us know when food is spoiled.

• What are your favorite things to smell?
• What smell do you dislike the most?
• What do we do to smell nice?

OUR EYES

With our eyes we see the world.
They are colored brown or blue,
Hazel, green, or even black.
All of us are blessed with two.

Eyes can smile, blink, and wink,
Show we're sad, for then they weep.
All day long eyes work for us
And only close when we're asleep.

"Apple of my eye" God calls us.
Don't know just what that is?
It means God likes us lots and lots.
Aren't we lucky we are his?

WE TALK

Our eyes are precious.

- What beautiful things have you seen?
- What do people who can't see well need?
- How can you take care of your eyes?

SUNSHINE

Daddy calls me sunshine.
He says he likes my smile.
It brightens up his day
And cheers him up a while.

Mommy calls me sunshine
When I am extra good
And help her with the baby
Or do just what I should.

Brother (sister) calls me sunshine
On days I'm not a pest
And leave his (her) things alone
And don't disturb his (her) rest.

Jesus calls me sunshine.
His love shines out through me.
When I make people happy,
He loves me 'specially.

WE TALK

We give one another special names or nicknames.

• What is your nickname?
• What are the nicknames for others in your family?
• What can you do to be sunshine in your family?

Taking Care of Me

A splendid gift God gave to me.
Can you guess what it could be?
All have one including you.
Here are things that it can do:

Hop and skip and run a race,
Fly a kite and make a face,
Sing a song and tell a joke,
Dance a jig and smile at folk,
Hear a story and bake a cake,
Build a fort, swim in a lake,
Paint a picture, throw a ball,
Give a hug, and that's not all.
Eat dessert and play all day,
Watch TV and kneel to pray.

Now you know without a doubt.
My body's what this poem's about:
Skin and hands and heart and nose.
Eyes and ears and head and toes!
Caring for this gift's a way
To thank God for it every day.
Here are caring things I do.
Hope you always do them too.

Brush my teeth and wash my hands,
Dress as warm as weather demands,
Eat the food Mom says is good,
Go to bed the time I should,
Take a bath and keep from danger,
Never go with any stranger,
Play outside, and when I'm sick,
Do what helps me get well quick.

WE TALK

God loves you and wants you to take care of yourself.

• What about your body makes you happy or thankful?
• How can you take better care of your body?

Sharing Poem

Pat thighs and clap hands in each refrain.

When we're munching on a treat
And our friend has none to eat,
What do we do?

Refrain: We [pat] share. [pat, clap, clap]
          We [pat] share. [pat, clap, clap]

When we're paging through a book
And our sister wants a look,
What do we do?

Refrain: We [pat] share. [pat, clap, clap]
          We [pat] share. [pat, clap, clap]

When we're watching the TV
And there's a show Dad wants to see,
What do we do?

Refrain: We [pat] share. [pat, clap, clap]
          We [pat] share. [pat, clap, clap]

When we're bouncing a new ball
And someone's playing not at all,
What do we do?

Refrain: We [pat] share. [pat, clap, clap]
         We [pat] share. [pat, clap, clap]

When we're playing with a toy
And here comes a girl or boy
What do we do?

Refrain: We [pat] share. [pat, clap, clap]
         We [pat] share. [pat, clap, clap]

WE TALK

Jesus wants us to love one another. Sharing is one way to
show our love.

• When has someone shared with you?
• How did it make you feel?
• When have you shared with someone?
• How did sharing make you feel?

My Friends

I like my friends,
Both girls and boys.
We run in the sun
And play with toys,
Take turns in games,
And like to share.
When I am sad,
They show they care.

Each night I pray
When day is done
That God will bless them,
Every one.

WE TALK

Friends are a gift.

• Who are your friends?
• What do you like to do with your friends?
• How do you make friends?
• How do you show that you are a good friend?

FEELINGS

When I'm angry, you can tell:
I stamp my feet and frown and yell. [Stamp feet.]

When I'm sad, I mope about:
I sigh and cry and don't go out.
[Put hands under chin, cupping face.]

When I'm scared by day or night,
I shake and hide, my eyes closed tight. [Shake.]

When I'm happy, I whistle and sing.
I laugh at almost anything.
[Extend arms to sides.]

Whether I'm feeling good or bad,
God loves me and for this I'm glad! [Clap.]

WE TALK

Feelings are normal. Sometimes we express them through words, but sometimes we use sounds and actions.

• What makes you happy?
• What makes you sad?
• What makes you afraid?
• Who can you talk to when you are sad or afraid?

I'm Growing Up

I am growing older,
And this is how I know:
Each year on my birthday
Another candle glows.

I am growing taller,
Not as tall as trees,
But now I come up higher
Than my father's knees.

I am growing wider,
And I no longer fit
In the baby's highchair
Where I used to sit.

I am growing heavy,
Or so my mother said
Last evening when she picked me up
To carry me to bed.

I am growing smarter.
I can count to three,
And sometimes I can even
Say some of my ABC's.

I am growing stronger,
Stronger day by day.
I can help to clean our house
And put my things away.

I am growing bigger,
Bigger than my clothes.
At least my skin still fits me
From my fingers to my toes!

WE TALK

God gave you a mind so you can think.

• How high can you count?
• What new things have you learned?
• What would you like to learn?

Good Words

A word is such a mighty thing.
Some words soothe, and some words sting.
Gentle words can calm your fears
They can even stop your tears.

Some words make you very glad,
Others make you sad or mad.
Speaking words polite and kind
Brings smiles to faces you will find.

I'd like to offer, if I may,
A few good words for you to say.
To start the day a pleasant way.
Greet "Good morning," "Have a good day."

Say "Can I help?" if you are able,
"Excuse me" when burping
or leaving the table.

When passing a person or stepping on toes,
"Pardon me" is proper, as everyone knows.

"Good luck" is how to cheer people on.
"Congrats" is due after they've won.
Say "God bless you" when people sneeze.
To ask for something, always say "Please."

If you make a mistake, apologize.
Saying "I'm sorry" is healthy and wise.
When someone says, "I'm sorry," to you.
"I forgive you" makes things like new.

"Thank you," "You're welcome"
we must not forget.
But we're not finished. There's one more yet.
Best of all and important too
Are the three little words, "I love you."

WE TALK

Saying nice things to others shows that we care about them.

- When has someone said something nice to you?
  How did it make you feel?
- What good words in this poem will you try
  to say more often?

FAMILY LAUGHS

My mother usually giggles.
The baby squeals with glee.
My father laughs so much he shakes.
Aunt Rose just goes, "Tee hee."

I laugh so much I hurt.
I laugh until I cry.
I laugh so hard I roll on the ground.
Sometimes I don't even know why.

WE TALK

Have you ever heard an animal laugh? People laugh in many different ways and for different reasons.

- What are some things that make you laugh?
- How can you make someone laugh?
- Who do you like to hear laugh?

MY FATHER

My father is so very good.
He works and keeps our home nice too.
He helps me dress the way I should,
And tells me what I ought to do.

My father is a lot of fun.
He likes to tease and tickle me.
We fly our kite, play ball, and run.
My favorite place is on his knee.

My father is so very smart.
When I ask, "Why?" he answers me.
I love my dad with all my heart.
For he's the best. Don't you agree?

WE TALK

Fathers are all different. Jesus called God his Father.

• What do you like about your father?
• What does your father do for you?

A FAMILY TALE

Kitty Cat and Tom, her brother,
Came home from school.
Mr. Cat was cooking dinner.
Mom sat on a stool.
"Oh, no!" meowed little Kitty Cat.
"I think I lost a mitten."
Her whiskers twitched. Her eyes filled up.
She sniffed. Poor little kitten.

"Don't cry, my dear," said Kitty's mom.
"It's no catastrophe."
Tom purred, "Don't worry. I'll go back
And see where it can be."
Mom gave Kitty catnip,
And Dad made her some tea.
He said, "Tom might find your mitten.
Let's just wait and see."

Through some catalogs they looked.
One mitten no one sold.
Searching through the ragbag,
They found one much too old.
Tom returned with empty paws.
No mitten could he find.
"I'll knit a mitten," Mom declared,
"And make it the same kind."

So a mitten for her kitten
Mother sat and knit.
When Kitty tried it on,
It was a PURRfect fit.
"Oh, thank you, Mom," she said
And gave her a big hug.
Then ready for a catnap,
Kitty curled up on the rug.

WE TALK

Family members help one another.

- When has your family helped you?
- How have you helped someone in your family?
- When do you pray for your family members?

My Angel

I have my very own angel
Who's with me night and day.
Although I cannot see him,
I know he helps me pray.
He also keeps me safe
And tells me what to do.
He prays for me so someday
I'll be in heaven too.

WE TALK

God gave you your guardian angel.
You can ask your angel to help you to be good.

- When would it be especially good
  to pray to your angel?
- What would you say to your angel
  when you get up in the morning?
- What would you say to your angel
  when you go to bed?

GOD AND GOD'S FAMILY

God Is There

Child repeats the sentences printed in **bold**.

When I run in the sun,
God is there. **God is there.**
When I fall playing ball,
God cares. **God cares.**
When I'm sad or I'm glad.
God knows. **God knows.**
When I mind or I'm kind,
God sees. **God sees.**
God is with me day and night,
Helping me to do what's right.
I love you, God. **I love you, God!**

WE TALK

God, like air, can't be seen. But God is everywhere.
He is always with us.

- How is God a loving Father to you?
- When can you talk to God?
- What can you say to God?

GOD'S FAMILY

To the tune of "Row, Row, Row Your Boat"

Women, men, girls, and boys,
[Point to several people.]
Mary, saints, and me—
[Point up and then to self.]
All are members of God's church.
[Extend arms wide.]
We're God's family.
[Clap twice at end.]

WE TALK

All of the members of the church are our brothers and sisters. God is our Father. We care for and pray for one another.

• When did you become a member of God's family?
• Who are some other members of God's family?
• Who in God's family needs your prayers today?

God Loves Me

God loves me,
[Clap, clap, point to self.]
And I love you.
[Clap, clap, point forwards.]
We show love
[Clap, clap, fold hands over heart.]
By what we do.
[Clap, clap, hold out hands.]

WE TALK

Saying I love you isn't enough. We must show people we love them.

• How can you show you love God?
• How can you show you love other people?

MOTHER MARY

Mary, girl of Galilee,
Was holy as no other.
Always gentle, kind, and loving,
She was the perfect mother.

When Angel Gabriel asked her
If she would have God's Son,
Mary didn't think twice.
She said, "Let it be done."

So now we honor Mary,
God's mother and ours too,
And try like her to say yes
To what we're meant to do.

WE TALK

Mary always listened to God. She said yes to God's plan to
be the mother of Jesus. This was not easy.

• What does God ask you to do?
• How do you honor Mary?

The Holy Family

Jesus, Mary, Joseph
Lived in Galilee.
They seemed to all the neighbors
A normal family.

Mary, Jesus' mother,
Worked hard all day long:
Baked bread, sewed clothes, fetched water.
She often sang a song.

Joseph, Mary's husband,
Loved her and her boy.
By working as a carpenter,
He cared for them with joy.

Jesus was a good son.
He did as he was told
And helped his mom and Joseph
Until he was quite old.

But Jesus, Mary, and Joseph
Were a special three,
For Jesus was God's Son
In the Holy Family.

WE TALK

Being holy is doing what we are supposed to do
and being loving.

• What holy things did Mary, Joseph, and Jesus do?
• What holy things can you do in your family?

Saint Joseph

When God was looking for a man
To be a father to his Son,
He thought a Jewish carpenter
Named Joseph would be just the one.

Now Joseph made a super dad,
For he was always just and good.
With Mary, he raised Jesus well
And taught him how to work with wood.

Because Saint Joseph was the head
Of Jesus' family from its birth,
In heaven he still guards and helps
The family Jesus has on earth.

WE TALK

Saint Joseph was known as a good man. He is the patron of the church. This means he prays for us.

• What do you think Joseph did for Jesus and Mary?
• When would you pray to Saint Joseph?

In Church

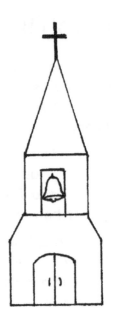

In God's holy house
I'm as quiet as can be.
There I talk to Jesus,
And Jesus talks to me.

Church, God's holy house,
Is not the place for fun.
I do not laugh or giggle,
Wiggle, scream, or run.

Deep within my heart
When I'm very, very still,
I hear God say, "I love you,
And I always will."

WE TALK

God is present in a special way in church. There his family comes together to worship him.

- What is the name of your church?
- What do you like about your church?

HEAVEN

Heaven is an awesome place
Where I'll see God face to face,
Live with Jesus, Mary, too,
Angels, saints, and, I hope, you.
I'll go there if I am good
And love all others as I should.

WE TALK

In heaven we will be happy forever.

• Who do you know who is in heaven?
• What would you say to God when you get to heaven?
• What good act could you do today?

THE WORLD

WHAT GOD MADE

God made the sun and the great blue sky.
[Make a circle with arms; open and raise hands.]

God made the stars and the moon.
[Open and close fingers.]

God made lakes and birds that fly.
[Flap arms.]

God made the little raccoon.
[Make circles with fingers around eyes.]

God made mountains and green, grassy hills.
[Make a peak with hands.]

God made the fish in the sea.
[Put palms together and wiggle hands forward.]

God made flowers like daffodils.
[Pretend to smell a flower.]

But best of all, God made me!
[Point to self.]

WE TALK

God is almighty. He made everything out of nothing.

• What works of God do you especially like?
• What can you say to God for making you?

THE DAYS OF CREATION

To the tune of "The Twelve Days of Christmas"

The first day of creation
[Hold up one finger.]
God made the light so bright.
[Open and close hands like a blinking light.]
And everything was oh so good.
[Rotate arms around each other
and then extend hands to sides.]

The second day of creation
[Hold up two fingers.]
God made the sky so high.
[Point up.]
And everything was oh so good.
[Rotate arms, extend hands.]

The third day of creation
[Hold up three fingers.]
God made the earth and sea.
[Join hands to form a ball;
move right arm in a wave movement.]
And everything was oh so good.
[Rotate arms, extend hands.]

The fourth day of creation
[Hold up four fingers.]
Sun, moon, and stars God made.
[Make a high sweeping motion
writh right arm.]
And everything was oh so good.
[Rotate arms, extend hands.]

The fifth day of creation
[Hold up five fingers.]
God made the birds and fish.
[Wave hands at side; put hands together
and move them from side to side.]
And everything was oh so good,
[Rotate arms, extend hands.]

The sixth day of creation
[Hold up six fingers.]
God made the beasts and us.
[Point to self.]
And everything was very, very good.
[Rotate arms, extend hands.]

The seventh day, work ended,
[Hold up seven fingers.]
God took a little rest,
[Rest head on hands.]
So Sunday's the best day and most blessed.
[Put palms together.]

WE TALK

On Sunday we praise and thank God for all his gifts.

• What does your family do to make Sunday special?
• What can you do to care for God's gifts?

Baby Chick

A baby chick came out of an egg—
[Make a fist and break through it with the other hand.]
Its beak, its head, a wing, then a leg.
It greeted me with a "peep, peep, peep."
Then nodded its head and went to sleep.
[Fold hands at side of head.]

WE TALK

We celebrate Easter with Easter eggs. This is because, just as a chick comes out of an egg, Jesus came out of his tomb with new life.

• Did you ever watch an egg hatch? If so, what was it like?
• How does your family decorate Easter eggs?

Buttercup

In the soil, dark and deep,
Lies a seed fast asleep.
Sun and rain wake it up.
It grows to be a buttercup.
In this little yellow flower,
We can see God's love and power.

WE TALK

God gave us flowers to make the world more beautiful.

- What other flowers can you name?
- What do flowers need to grow?

A Fish

Put hands together with thumbs crossed and "swim."

I am a fish in the great blue sea.
God made me as happy as can be.
I swim all day and sleep all night.
To be God's fish is my delight.

WE TALK

Jesus told his fisherman friends to catch people for him, that is, to lead them to Jesus.

• Who led you to Jesus?
• How can you show you are happy to be a child of God?

MUSIC

We hear music everywhere,
Even in church where it's a prayer.
Songs can make me want to dance,
Which I do when there's the chance.
Some are sad and some are sweet.
To peppy ones I tap my feet,
Clap my hands, and sing along.
Sometimes I just hum a song.
I can whistle some tunes too.
I like music. How about you?

WE TALK

We praise God when we sing in church.

- When else do you sing?
- What is your favorite song?
- What instrument would you like to play?

BIRDS

I love to watch God's birds fly by,
Gliding smoothly in the sky.

God gives them bugs and worms to eat
Because for them they are a treat.

Sometimes God sends rainy weather
So they can wash each pretty feather.

God gives them for their families
Cozy nests in tall green trees.

All things are from God above,
Who cares for birds and us with love.

WE TALK

Birds learn to fly and act like birds from their parents.

- How do you parents care for you and teach you?
- What kind of birds do you see in your neighborhood?

COLORS

Red, red — roses are red.
Red is the hair on Jeremy's head.
Cherries are red and strawberries too.
I like red apples. How about you?

Orange, orange — oranges are orange.
I'd like one now — I certainly would!
A gorgeous orange is the setting sun.
I think orange is a lot of fun.

Yellow, yellow — butter is yellow.
So is the cap on that little fellow.
Bees and lemons, bananas, the sun.
Want a happy color? Yellow's the one.

Green, green — grass is green.
Trees and leaves — a lovely scene.
Lettuce, peas, and beans and such.
God must like green very much.

Blue, blue — the sky is blue —
Light blue, dark blue, dazzling blue too.
Bluebirds and blueberries, oceans and lakes.
The hue of blue a pretty world makes.

Brown, brown — mud is brown.
Mud on the rug make Mom and Dad frown.
Brown is the color of things that are nice
Like chocolate, puppies, birds, and mice.

Purple, purple — grapes are fine.
Pansies, violets, clouds, and wine.
Pale and soft or deep and rich,
Purple's my favorite. I will not switch.

WE TALK

God is good to put colors in our world.

- What is your favorite color?
- What colors are not named in the poem?
- What do you use to make colored pictures?

A Raindrop

[Tap two fingers on palm of other hand.]
Pitter-patter, pitter-patter
On my windowpane.
Downpour, drizzle, shower, no matter:
I love to watch it rain.

If I could be a raindrop,
Do you know what I'd do?
I'd join the mighty ocean
For ships to sail through.

Or I might be a river,
A creek, a spring, or lake,
So on a summer's day
A swim in me you'd take.

[Rub palms together to make a swishing sound.]
Or to your house I'd flow
Into your tub and sink.
Perhaps I'd fill a glass
So you could have a drink.

But then I like to think
I'd soak the ground below
So thirsty grass and flowers
Can live, be green, and grow.

[Pat thighs, alternating.]
Or else I'd make a puddle
Where you can play and splash
Or a pond for fish and frogs
Where birds can take a bath.

Maybe if I'm lucky,
As a waterfall I'd thunder
And be a thing of beauty
Where people stand in wonder.

[Tap two fingers on palm of other hand.]
A baptismal font is where
I'd like the most to be.
For then I'd help a person
Join God's family.
Pitter-patter, pitter-patter
Plink, plink, plink.

WE TALK

We need water to live.

• How does your family use water?
• How can you avoid wasting water?
• When do you play in water?

ANIMALS

Earth is like a great big zoo
Filled with creatures God has made
In many sizes, colors, and shapes.
Let's imagine their parade.

First come the kittens followed by puppies,
Long-necked giraffes,
and then braying donkeys,
Possums and zebras
with black and white stripes,
Tigers and bears, and chattering monkeys,

Hopping frogs and slithering snakes.
Roaring lions and rhinoceroses,
Sharp-toothed beavers, turtles with shells,
Porcupines, hippopotamuses,

Horses, cows, and woolly sheep,
Kangaroos and antlered deer,
Moles and moose and naughty mice,
Waddling penguins, wolves, and steer,

Crocodiles and alligators,
Otters, gerbils, masked raccoons,
Leopards, lemurs, lizards, llamas,
Bleating goats, and big baboons,

Lazy sloths, coyotes too,
Hamsters, pigs, odd platypuses,
Sneaky foxes, squirrels, hyenas,
Rabbits, weasels, walruses,

Long-tongued anteaters, cheetahs, chickens,
Gorillas, gophers, buffalo,
Two-humped camels, yaks, and panthers,
Then the snails moving slow,

Bringing up the very end,
Elephants with waving trunks,
Far behind and being kind
Come the cute but stinky skunks,

Creatures living in the sea,
Birds and bugs all fit this list.
But the mighty dinosaurs,
Thank the Lord, no more exist!

WE TALK

God is very smart to make so many different animals.

- How do animals help us?
- Where can you see animals?
- If you could be an animal, which one would you be? Why?

BUTTERFLY

A fat, striped caterpillar
Crawled up a tree.
[Inch right forefinger up left arm from elbow to thumb.]
He stopped at a twig
To start his mystery.

A case formed around him
[Wrap right hand around forefinger.]
He hung there in the air.
'Til he became a butterfly,
[Repeatedly press right hand's thumb
and forefinger together.]
A beauty, I declare!

And now the caterpillar
Had wings and could fly.
For us he stands for Easter
And here's the reason why.

A tomb held Jesus' body,
But like the butterfly,
He came out with better life
And so will you and I.

WE TALK

A caterpillar doesn't know that he will be a beautiful butterfly. But we know we will have new life someday.

- How is a butterfly different from a caterpillar?
- Why do you see butterflies on flowers?
- How do we celebrate Jesus rising from the dead?

BIBLE STORIES

GOD'S BOOK

God wrote a great big book for me.
The Bible is its name.
Though it has many different parts,
God's message is the same.

In story after story
From beginning to the end,
I hear God speaking to my heart,
"I love you, my dear friend."

WE TALK

The Bible is holy because God is the author.
It tells us about Jesus.

• Where do you hear the Bible read?
• What are your favorite Bible stories?
• What do you know about Jesus?

God's Care

"Don't you worry," Jesus says.
"See the birds up in the sky.
They don't plant or harvest crops,
Yet they have a food supply."

"See the flowers in the field.
They don't sew and make their clothes.
Yet a king in all his glory
Isn't dressed as fine as those."

"God takes care of birds and flowers.
He cares for you, his child, too,
And even knows how many hairs
Are on your head." Do you?

WE TALK

God takes care of everything he made.

• What do birds eat?
• What are some beautiful flowers?
• Why shouldn't you worry?

ABRAHAM

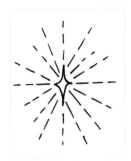

How many stars in the sky?
How many sands on the shore?
How many offspring would Abraham have?
God said he'd have even more!

Abraham had not even one son,
And Sarah his wife was quite old.
But they had a boy from whom hundreds more came
Just as God had foretold.

Hundreds and hundreds of years went by.
Then Abraham's family gave birth
To Jesus, the Savior and Mary's Son:
God who had come down to earth.

WE TALK

Abraham was the first person to believe in one God.
He had great trust in God.

• How has God been good to you?
• What promise to Abraham did God keep?

Moses

God's people, the Hebrews, as slaves in Egypt
    Suffered horribly.
When Pharaoh ordered their baby boys killed,
    They longed even more to be free.

A baby named Moses was placed in a basket
    And hidden in reeds on the water.
One day he was found, saved, and adopted
    By none other than Pharaoh's daughter.

Moses grew up and was watching some sheep
    When he saw something odd.
A bush was on fire but not burning up.
    Then came the voice of God.

"Go, Moses, to Pharaoh and give him this message:
    'Let all of my people go free.'"
Moses obeyed, but Pharaoh did not
    'Till ten plagues made him finally agree.

That night the Hebrews hurried to pack.
    They ate herbs and lamb and then fled.
As they escaped, God led his people
    As fire and a cloud at the head.

Oh, no! An army was rapidly following.
    Pharaoh had changed his mind.
The Red Sea blocked the Hebrews' way
    The enemy closed in from behind.

Their horses and chariots drew ever nearer.
    The Hebrews were terrified.
Moses lifted his staff, stretched his hand o'er the sea.
    The waters began to divide.

All during the night a mighty wind blew,
    Cutting a path in the sea.
The Hebrews walked bravely through walls of water
    On sand that was dry as could be.

As soon as the people had all safely passed.
    They heard a rush and a roar.
The water flowed back and stopped Pharaoh's army.
    Their God had helped them once more.

With Moses as leader, the Hebrews walked on.
    God fed them with manna and quail.
He led them to water and gave them ten laws.
    With his help they could not fail.

It took forty years for God's people to enter
    Canaan, the promised land.
Always remember when you are in trouble,
    Your God is close at hand.

WE TALK

God saved the Hebrews and gave them land. He saved us
by sending Jesus and giving us heaven.

• In what ways did God help his people?
• How does God help you?

JONAH

God said to Jonah,
"Go, go, go." [Point.]
But Jonah thought,
"No, no, no." [Shake head.]

He hid on a ship.
Row, row, row. [Make rowing motions.]
And winds began to
Blow, blow, blow. [Cup hands at mouth.]

"It's my fault," said Jonah.
"Oh, oh, oh. [Throw up arms.]
Throw me overboard.
Woe, woe, woe."
[Put hands to head. Shake head.]

A big fish ate him.
Yum, yum, yummy. [Lick lips.]
Jonah lived three days in his
Tum, tum, tummy. [Pat stomach.]

To the enemy land Jonah
Came, came, came. [March in place.]
He preached to the people,
"Shame, shame, shame." [Shake forefinger.]

The people turned good.
Yay, yay, yay! [Wave fists in air.]
But Jonah was surprised.
Hey, hey, hey. [Raise hands palms upturned.]

God sent a plant to
Grow, grow, grow. [Stoop and rise.]
Jonah was happy.
Ho, ho, ho. [Rock back and forth.]

A worm ate the plant.
Chomp, chomp, chomp. [Chew.]
And Jonah was angry.
Stomp, stomp, stomp. [Stomp.]

"See," said God, "you loved
One, one, one. [Hold up one finger.]
But I love everyone
Under the sun!" [Extend arms wide.]

WE TALK

God always forgives us when we are sorry.

• What did Jonah do wrong?
• How can you show God you are sorry after you have
  done something wrong?

DAVID

When God ordered Samuel to find a new king.
He visited Jesse, whose sons numbered eight.
The first seven came to him one at a time.
None would be king, but then Jesse said, "Wait!
David, my youngest, is guarding my sheep."

This son was handsome, courageous, and sharp.
God chose him king, and he went to the palace
To cheer up King Saul just by playing the harp.

An enemy soldier, the giant Goliath,
Said, "I'll fight one person. Does anyone dare?"
No one was willing, so David said, "I do.
I've already killed both a lion and a bear."

A slingshot and five stones were all the lad had
While Goliath wore armor and carried a spear.
But David was armed with a great trust in God.
With only one stone shot, the victory was clear.

The giant Goliath lay dead on the ground.
After winning more wars, David ruled as the king,
United two kingdoms and then left behind
A hundred and fifty songs we still sing.

WE TALK

Jesus was born from King David's family. His songs — or psalms — are in the Bible.

• Why did young David win the fight with Goliath?
• When do we sing David's songs?

Jesus and the Children

Jesus had a hard day.
He sat down to rest.
Parents brought their children,
Hoping they'd be blessed.

But the twelve apostles
Told them, "Go away!"
Then Jesus wasn't happy.
He said, "Have them stay."

"Let the children come here.
Don't ever stop them, please,
For my Father's kingdom is
For little ones like these."

Jesus hugged the children
And blessed each girl and boy.
They left then with their parents,
Their hearts were full of joy.

WE TALK

Jesus is a friend to children.

• How do you know that Jesus loves you?
• How can you show Jesus that he is your friend?

The Daughter of Jairus

A little girl was dying.
Her dad knew what to do.
He hurried to get Jesus
Who'd healed more than a few.

"Come, Jesus, help my daughter,"
The man named Jairus said.
They headed toward his home
Where the girl lay sick in bed.

A messenger told Jairus,
"Too late. Your girl has died."
"Don't worry. Just believe.
She'll live," the Lord replied.

At the house of Jairus
Everyone was weeping.
They laughed when Jesus said,
"She's not dead but sleeping."

Then Jesus took her hand
And ordered, "Child, arise!"
At once the girl got up
To everyone's surprise.

How happy were the parents
To see her on her feet.
Then Jesus kindly told them,
"Now find her food to eat."

WE TALK

Jesus loves people and helps them.

• How does Jesus help people in this story?
• How do you think the girl's parents felt after Jesus' visit?
• When can you ask Jesus to help you?

A Good Samaritan

One day a man was traveling
    To another town.
Some robbers came and beat him up
    And left him on the ground.

A man who came along the road
    Passed the man right by.
A second man also came that way
    And left him there to die.

The third man was a Samaritan —
    He was an enemy.
But when he saw the poor man bleed,
    He was kind as kind could be.

He bandaged all the man's deep wounds
    And took him to an inn.
He sat beside him all night long
    And paid for both of them.

To understand what Jesus means
    By loving one another
Just think of the Samaritan
    Who showed love like a brother.

WE TALK

We call people who do good deeds Good Samaritans.

• Why do you think the first two men didn't help
  the beaten man?
• What good deeds did the Samaritan do?
• Who has been a Good Samaritan to you?

Five Loaves and Two Fish

All the lad had were five loaves and two fish.
[Show five fingers on one hand and two on the other.]
Meant to take home as a family dish.

When feeding five thousand was Jesus' wish,
[Show five fingers on one hand.]
The boy handed over five loaves and two fish.
[Show five fingers on one hand and two on the other.]

Working six months of the year would not make
[Show six fingers.]
Money enough for the food it would take
To feed such a crowd, but now Jesus had
Five loaves and two fish from the generous lad.
[Show five fingers on one hand and two on the other.]

People sat down, and then Jesus prayed grace,
Passed out some bread and some fish at each place.
Everyone ate as much as they wished
Thanks to the gift of five loaves and two fish.
[Show five fingers on one hand and two on the other.]

"Gather the leftovers," Jesus then said.
His followers filled up
twelve baskets with bread.
[Show ten fingers and then two.]

Jesus that day was the cause of much joy
Because of five loaves and two fish from one boy.
[Show five fingers on one hand and two on the other.]

5 + 2 = ?

WE TALK

Jesus felt sorry for the hungry people. He feels sorry for hungry people today.

• What does it feel like to be hungry?
• How did the boy help Jesus?
• How can you be like the boy and help feed others?

SPECIAL DAYS

ADVENT

Hush! The world is waiting,
[Raise finger to lips.]
Waiting for Baby Jesus.
[Rock arms.]

Mary and Joseph are waiting,
[Extend one arm, then the other.]
Waiting for Mary's Son.
[Rock arms.]

Shepherds and kings are waiting,
[Extend one arm, then the other.]
Waiting for the newborn king.
[Rock arms.]

I am waiting,
[Point to self.]
Waiting for my Savior.
[Extend arms up.]

WE TALK

During the four weeks before Christmas, we prepare to celebrate the birth of Jesus.

• What can you do to prepare your heart for Jesus?
• Why is Jesus better than Santa Claus?

Saint Nicholas

To the tune of "Jolly Old Saint Nicholas"

Holy, kind Saint Nicholas,
Friendly, good, and wise —
When he could, he helped the poor
Sometimes by surprise.

We can be like Nicholas
And have a lot of fun,
Showing by our words and deeds
Love for everyone.

WE TALK

The feast of Saint Nicholas is December 6. He was a bishop who gave three poor sisters the money they needed to get married.

- Why on the night of December 5 do some children put their shoes out?
- How can you be like Saint Nicholas?

CHRISTMAS BELLS

[Mime pulling on a bell rope throughout the poem.]

Ring the bells on Christmas morn.
Tell the news that Jesus is born.
Ring them far. Ring them near.
Ring them loud for all to hear.
Over the world let them sing,
Ding, dong, ding, dong, ding, dong, ding.

WE TALK

Bells make pretty music. They call people to church to pray.
They are also rung for special celebrations.

• Why are we happy on Christmas morning?
• When do you hear the church bells ringing?
• Why do you think that God came to earth as a baby?

CHRISTMAS JOY

Baby sleeping on the hay,
Peacefully in Bethlehem's cave,
Came to us from heaven that day.
Gift from God the world to save.

Mother Mary smiles with joy.
Joseph's standing by.
Shepherds come to see the boy,
Sent by angels in the sky.

Guided by a special star,
Wise men travel from afar,
Searching for the newborn king.
Precious gifts for him they bring.

On Christmas Day we celebrate
The birth of Jesus our Lord.
I'm so happy I can't wait
I'll twirl and dance and clap and cheer.
Right now!
[Twirl, dance, clap, or cheer.]

WE TALK

We set up scenes of the first Christmas in church and in our homes. They are called nativity sets.

- Who do you see in a nativity set?
- What else do you see?

VALENTINE

Because you mean so much to me,
I give this valentine to you.
It says I love you with all my heart.
I hope you love me too.

WE TALK

February 14 is the feast of Saint Valentine. On this day we give cards and candy to people we love. God loves you more than anyone else loves you.

• To whom would you give a Valentine?
• Who loves you? How do you know?

Saint Patrick's One God

Saint Patrick lived in Ireland.
A very smart bishop was he.
He used a three-leaf clover
To teach the Trinity.

Father, Son, and Holy Spirit,
These Persons total three.
But like a three-leaf clover
They're one — a mystery!

WE TALK

We believe in one God, but there are three Persons in God.
We will never completely understand this.

• What things on earth are hard to understand?
• Which Person of the Trinity do you speak to most?
• How do you make the Sign of the Cross?

Easter Cheer

I live.
[Point to self.]

You live.
[Point forwards.]

We'll all live forever.
[Sweep arm across front.]

Jesus died and rose to life.
[Stoop and rise.]

We'll live with him forever.
Yay, Jesus!
[Jump and wave arms in the air.]

WE TALK

Every living being dies. After Jesus died, he came out of his tomb with new and glorious life. He promised that we will have this kind of life too someday.

• Why was it a surprise that Jesus rose from the dead?
• Do you look forward to heaven? Why?

NEW LIFE

Jesus is risen.
[Take two steps forward on the beats.]
Al-le-lu-ia!
[Raise arms up and down twice.]

Jesus is risen.
[Take two steps backward on the beats.]
Al-le-lu-ia!
[Raise arms up and down twice.]

Jesus is risen.
[Take two steps forward on the beats.]
Al-le-lu-ia!
[Raise arms up and down twice.]

That's gr—rr—
[Swing right arm around twice
as if winding up for a pitch.] —eat!
[Jerk right elbow back. Clap twice.]

WE TALK

Alleluia means "praise God." It is a word that shows joy and victory.

• Why do you especially say alleluia at Easter?
• How do you celebrate Easter?

THANKSGIVING

Thank you, God, for things I hear:
[Cup ears with hands.]
Ringing bells and chirping birds,
Lively songs and loving words.

Thank you, God, for things I smell:
[Touch nose.]
Fresh cut grass and homemade bread,
Flowers, popcorn, a baby's head.

Thank you, God, for things I feel:
[Open hands wide.]
Gooey clay and furry cats,
Sunshine, tickling, hugs, and pats.

Thank you, God, for things I taste:
[Point to mouth.]
Pizza, bacon, cakes, and pies,
Jello, milkshakes, hot French fries.

Thank you, God, for things I see:
[Point to eyes.]
Stars and flowers, ships at sea,
Books and shows, my family.

Most of all I thank you, God,
That you thought of making me.
[Sweep hands down over body.]

WE TALK

George Washington, the first president of the United States,
declared the first Thanksgiving Day. Usually people gave
thanks to God for a good harvest. Nowadays we thank God
for every good thing.

• Why should we thank God?
• What do you especially thank God for?
• What are your favorite foods?

MY PRAYERS

Prayer Time

One, two:
    Here's what I do
Three, four:
    To love Jesus more.
Five, six:
    On him my heart fix.
Seven eight:
    Sit still and wait.
Nine, ten:
    Talk to my friend, Jesus.

WE TALK

Praying is talking to God and listening to God speak in our hearts. We can pray out loud or silently.

- What would you say to Jesus right now?
- What prayers do you know
  or would you like to know by heart?

Prayer in the Morning

Thank you, God, for the brand new day.
Help me live it as you say.
Now I give you all I'll do.
May it show my love for you.

Prayer at Night

Dear God, before I fall asleep,
I have some things to say.
I'm sorry for the times I failed
To love and to obey.
I thank you for the good things
That happened all day through.
Please bless my family and my friends.
And make me more like you.

WE TALK

It's good to speak to God first thing in the morning and at night before you go to bed.

- How can you remember to pray morning and night?
- When else can you pray?

Good Shepherd

O Jesus, Good Shepherd,
You watch from above.
You know me by name
And call me with love.

You guard me from evil
And help me do right.
You guide me to safety
By day and by night.

You love and you care,
And give all that I need.
This day and always
I'll go where you lead.

WE TALK

Jesus called himself the Good Shepherd. We are like his
sheep. He loves and protects us.

• What does a shepherd do for his sheep?
• Where does Jesus lead us?
• How can you follow Jesus today?

WHAT I KNOW (PSALM 139)

O God, you know me through and through.
You know whenever I sit or stand.
You know my words before I do.
You read my mind. Oh, you're so grand!

You know whenever I go away
And when I'm sound asleep in bed.
You're all around me every day.
Your loving hand rests on my head.

If I would ever hide from sight
Above the sky, beneath the sea,
Far east or west, in dark of night.
I know you'd still be there for me.

WE TALK

This is a song prayer of King David in the Bible. It reminds us that God is always with us.

• What are some places where God is with you?
• How does it make you feel to know
  that God is always there?

To Mary

Mary, my mother in heaven above,
This day I thank you and show you my love.
Help me to grow up to be like your Son,
Kind and loving to everyone.

WE TALK

Mary loves you and cares about you. She wants you to be
with her and Jesus in heaven someday.

• How can you please God as Mary did?
• What prayers, hymns, and feast days give honor to Mary?